HOW TO LOVE SOMEONE TO DEATH

LOU BACON, M.ED.

Bloomington, IN  Milton Keynes, UK

authorHOUSE™

AuthorHouse™
1663 Liberty Drive,
Suite 200
Bloomington, IN 47403
www.authorhouse.com
Phone: 1-800-839-8640

AuthorHouse™ UK Ltd.
500 Avebury Boulevard
Central Milton Keynes, MK9 2BE
www.authorhouse.co.uk
Phone: 08001974150

First published by AuthorHouse 2/16/2006
ISBN: 1-4259-0324-X (sc)

Library of Congress Control Number: 2005910241

Printed in the United States of America
Bloomington, Indiana

This book is printed on acid-free paper.

ACKNOWLEDGEMENT

I would like to graciously thank the many souls who have taught me the art of living fully while sharing their end-of-life journey with me. To Dottie, Alex, Millie and Jeff, thank you for taking me right to the edge of the great abyss and allowing me to love and be loved in pure truth as I learned from you not to fear death, but instead, to respect and accept it's ultimate calling.

I thank my precious family, Don, Amanda and Cheyanne, for supporting my choice to enter the lives of those courageous souls who taught me how to reach beyond myself and uphold the dignity and nobility of so many that shared their end-of-days with me. This experience has forever changed my life and those who have loved me, with unconditional love, to serve and honor those in the process of dying.

TABLE OF CONTENTS

PREFACE

The truth is simple. Death and dying are frightening. Most of us are afraid to face death, as well as the process of dying. That's ok, as many of us are not taught very much about the concept of dying, or how to accept death, or even how to talk about it.

The offering of this book is to give the reader some simple guidance of how to approach your own process of loving someone to death. The focus of this book is on receiving the news that a person you love or care about has a terminal condition. When we receive the news that someone we care for has a terminal condition, we are first faced with concern for our Loved-one, and the discomfort of adjusting to the news. Then, we are faced with ourselves, and we start to ask the internal question of, "What do I do?"

Based on my experience of eleven years working as a direct-service volunteer for Hospice, I have often been asked, "How do you *do* that?" What the question refers too, is, how

I begin the practice of working on a most intimate level of caring for, and honoring the last remaining months, days and hours of life with an individual who is facing eminent death. This is not a manual or researched information from death-and-dying studies. This is simply what I know to be true of loving and caring for an individual during the last phase of life. This book is only meant to offer guidance based on very simple suggestions to help the reader open his or her mind and heart to the process of dying.

If you ever wondered what to do, or how to start caring for and supporting any individual who is going to die, this is what I know and what I have done, and what has served both my Loved-one, and myself. This offering is not complex, not difficult, and must be read with the understanding that what I have to offer is from my own personal experience of the dying process, that has helped me face many patients, friends and family members, with an open and loving heart so that their connection to me is one grounded in dignity, safety and truth. I love this work, and I believe in embracing the full experience of simply allowing that person who is moving away from life, to feel loved, honored and respected for who they are, no matter what physical, mental, emotional or spiritual state they are in. This is about simply loving ~

your Loved-one, and yourself.

When someone you love is faced with the reality that his or her life is going to end within a certain amount of time, it is a natural response to feel panic and fear. But there are steps you can take to rise above that fear. These steps are not difficult, but they do take time to learn.

The chapters in this book are based on personal insights from my experience working directly with patients as a hospice volunteer. These reflections of the work I have done with such special people that I have loved to death are written here to serve as tools for the reader. I hope that you find in these experiences, guidance that will allow you the courage and strength to use while taking time out of your own life, to love and support another human being to the end of theirs. These chapters provide gentle guidelines for you to read and think about in preparation for the time you will spend with a loved-one who is dying.

I cannot over emphasize how normal and okay it is to feel uncertain, or fearful about taking that step into the world of loss, and sharing the experience of watching a Loved-one leave this life. The experience at first can be very scary. It can be very painful. It can be very challenging. But believe this ~ as scary and as painful and as challenging as it can be, it can also be other things as well, such as a deepening of connection to your Loved-one, insight into your own personal strength and courage, and an enlightenment of truths – both spoken and unspoken, an awakening of your spirit, and most importantly, an expression of unconditional love that will envelope and comfort your Loved-one as he or she prepares to leave this life behind ~ and those other things are *well worth* the devotion and commitment it took to make the decision to do this.

For most of us, even for me from time to time, preparing for the death of a Loved-one is uncharted territory. Why? Because things change and shift moment to moment, day to day. The process here is dying, and dying takes on many shapes and forms, and everyone's experience is different. None of us can ever really be sure what will happen next, but remaining steady, present and committed, is the greatest gift you can possibly give your Loved-one at a time like this.

If you choose to begin this process, you will most certainly bring gifts of love and comfort to that special person you choose to be with at this time. But the gifts do not end with what you bring to your beloved. Once you step away, and time has taken that life away, you will discover a most amazing truth, as the end result has its own special quality and meaning. You will receive the gift of knowing. You will come away from this experience with greater insight not only of what you provided to your Loved-one, but insight into your *own* life from the experience of loving someone to death. You will see things differently for a while. You will have become opened to an experience that has allowed you to touch the life and end-of-days of someone special. That experience in and of itself, then becomes a gift to *you*. The gift of knowing that you helped another human being, through safe and loving guidance, continue the journey to go to the one place the living cannot go, to reach life's end.

Finding your center where you can quiet your mind and open your heart is the starting point for this work. There will be heartaches, fear and sadness. Yet trust, for there will *also* be discovery, joy (yes, joy), enlightenment, understanding and peace. There will be cascading emotions throughout this experience, and all of them will be worth every precious moment of your time. Start only with an understanding of this choice, of giving of your time and attention to the dying, and to opening your heart to love guiding you through this process, and you will then be prepared to receive the gift of love in return.

Introduction

Take a moment and just consider these questions...

What would you do if I were to tell you, that you had just 22 *months* left to live? I will help you try to answer that.... but because I am not you, I am sure I won't come up with everything that is going on inside of you. But for now, I will offer some fairly simple insights.

First you might think, "Well, that is almost two years." Yes, it is. You might start by thinking about the things you could do knowing that there are nearly two years left of your life, like the things you have always wanted to do, but never quite got around to doing. Ideas of traveling might begin to circulate, like where you would want to go, what cites, country sides, or beaches you would like to explore. Or, you might think about gatherings, outings, and social functions you have always wanted to attend. Perhaps you might focus on projects you would like to finish, or goals you still intend to reach by beginning something new.

What would you do if I were to tell you, that you had only 22 *weeks* left to live? Well, you might think of 22 weeks as nearly half a year. You might consider what it would be like to be spontaneous, driving away alone, or with a special person to share an adventure and seek out some excitement, or, privacy. Perhaps you might choose to seek solitude alone for a while as a reflective point from which to launch each new day. This might be a time when you decide to plan a party or personal gathering to say your "good-byes" to the people your have shared your life with. Maybe this time would offer you the chance to gather up some spectacular sunrises, or to look beyond the stars in the midnight sky.

What would you do if I were to tell you, that you only had 22 *days* left to live? Panic, probably. Would you look around and begin counting those people who were closest to your inner circle, and start reaching out just to hold on? Maybe you would imagine yourself wrapped up in soft, worn quilts, warm and stationary in the company of best friends or family sharing stories of your life. Would you treat yourself to the savory experience of your favorite foods, music, and written words? Perhaps you would choose to make all the arrangements of your own funeral service with lavish attention on all those things you once noticed were out of sync at other services you attended in the past.

What would you do if I were to tell you, that you only had 22 *hours* left to live? Go numb? Most likely. News like this is rarely received, yet my point here is simply this....**you never know**. It could even be 22 *minutes* from the moment you close this book, or from getting into the car, or taking out the trash....we just don't know. The point? Every moment does count, and it is up to us, and only us, to make them count.

For many of us, we are not typically taught how to embrace death. Yet death, in many places and at many, many times, is as present and demanding of our attention as any one of life's other events. Choosing to experience the dying process along side of a terminal Loved-one is an opportunity to face a great fear, one that takes courage and faith. In doing so, it *will* allow each of us to face that fear and begin passage into a greater understanding of who we are together *and* as individuals.

The offering of this book is to simply give you a gentle nudge onto the bridge that spans life and death. It sounds scary, I know. And it can be. The place of in-between, upon this bridge, is one where people learn so much about life and letting go of fear. It is a place where fear may hide and truth is present, where honesty breathes, acceptance grows and a place where love expands and thrives. It is a place of pure authenticity – love or fear – whatever is honest. Facing death with a willingness and openness of allowing life to move into death is the greatest most powerful expression of love. It allows whatever thoughts and emotions need to surface and to be witnessed as acceptable in that very moment where you and your Loved-one are. Facing death together, hand and hand, heart to heart, is about walking out on that bridge together, sharing the experience of uncertainly, dread as well as acceptance and grace. Yet in those moments, the bridge is never more powerful as it connects us to the ultimate truth of who we are, and how we love.

Loving Someone to Death is about loving not only the individual who is about to leave us through death, it is about loving ourselves in this same process. It is about facing fear head-on, with the express intention and belief that what we are about to give *and* receive, *will* be the result of a loving and accepting spirit that will only serve to strengthen our belief in humanity.

CHAPTER 1

THE LOVED ONE

Impending death comes in all shapes and sizes. It comes in every single age, color, gender, economic status, educational background and religious persuasion. Terminal illness can and often does, touch the lives of every individual on this planet. Reaching out to be there for someone during the final chapter of life, by nurturing, caring and healing is what this book is about, and with that in mind, I have chosen to refer to those persons who are faced with the end of their lives, as the Loved-one.

All through these chapters I will be offering guidance to the reader on what the needs of the Loved-one are, as well as how to examine and address your *own* needs. During the process of dying, our Loved-ones are *still* among the living and although they may appear different in some ways from what we were used too, they truly do, like every one of us, take comfort in the special bonds they share with those they care for and love. The terminally ill need love and goodness from those special individuals that they have loved, cared for, and trusted throughout their lives. It is my belief that we are all here to simply love, care for, and guide each other through all of life's doorways of experience. Throughout our life's journey we are continuously forging meaningful and lasting relationships with people we choose to open our minds and hearts too as an expression of our love.

Loving our Loved-ones to death, is purely an expression of our love to support them though whatever choices, beliefs, and wishes they express during this final stage of their lives. Each one of these special individuals offers us an opportunity to give and receive emotional, physical, and spiritual support. They are truly deserving of our complete attention as we share their last precious moments by honoring their changing needs as we prepare to say goodbye.

CHAPTER 2

THE BRIDGE

Throughout the chapters in this book, you will occasionally encounter references to *the bridge*. This is a metaphor that I have used for years to describe a part of the work I do with patients and Loved-ones I have chose to love to their deaths. I truly do believe that there is great honor in being there for anyone who is facing death, and my own personal thought process begins by traveling with them onto the bridge.

Let me begin by defining to you what this means to me, and then offer guidance to you so that you too, can build a bridge [of sorts] to strengthen your own personal experience while loving someone to death.

When you decide that you are going to share the passage of time with a Loved-one that is dying, the journey itself is very much like walking together upon a bridge. This bridge that I have chosen to walk onto is one I have created in my mind's eye. The concept of this bridge is a simple one that spans the uncharted place between life and death. Although constructed to support the weight of the dying process, the bridge is *still* a place of the living. It is a special place where two people come together to experience the intimacy of relationship while spanning, sharing, or reflecting in the waters of life's experience. Dying does not mean one is dead, it simply means that life is ending, and *that*, is a very important reality to behold. Being on the bridge is about living while dying is happening. It can be a difficult place at times, riddled with discomfort, confusion and uncertainty, but upon this bridge there is also wonder, meaning, and purpose of what the ending of life has to offer. The bridge offers a place to sit and bare witness to the ending of one person's life through reflecting, resolving, fearing, and loving by remaining open to the possibilities of understanding, acceptance, and growth. It is a place to offer quiet conversation or to simply honor silence. It is a place where two hearts and minds share stories, thoughts, worries, and joys. The bridge is a place where you and your Loved-one can laugh and sing or cry and anguish. It is a special place where two people meet to listen and breathe in the understanding of true companionship.

I offer you also, to take a moment and create an image that will have meaning and purpose to you while you share this journey. Most importantly it is a place that you create to keep this Loved-one safe and supported during the time you share together while life is ending. Stepping upon this bridge for you, is all about opening up to simply loving this person, fully, in whatever frame of mind and physical condition he or she is in. Here you offer a space that says you are present and attentive because you wish to be, and choose to remain a steady support while you follow the lead of your beloved while conversing or just being still.

Beneath the bridge flows the river of life's experience. This creative visual has helped me ease into the conversations about our lives where we might choose to sit and dangle our feet in the waters of story-telling while sharing another one of life's adventures. It is in this place ~ whether you think of it as a bridge, or a temple, or sanctuary ~ that trust and safety become the heart of the relationship. In my experience, I have offered a safe haven of confidentiality and truth with a Loved-one while sharing our hearts and our truths about who we are, what we have done and where we shall go. It is a mutual exchange, and one that is not always difficult, but often comforting because we both know that it is our last meeting place for a while, one we quietly embrace and appreciate while we have the time, even with words unspoken.

When the time I had spent together with those I have loved to death ended, and death arrived, we both departed from the bridge in opposite directions ~ that was an understanding I accepted from the start, and hopefully that too will be your realization as you begin this journey. From the moment I had stepped onto the bridge, I knew, without either one of us mentioning it, that we would not be leaving this sacred place together. Often times you will find, that there are no words to define this process, it is only a language of the heart. This profound realization often delivers a powerful impact, but one necessary as it too is a part of this process of choice and discovery.

The bridge is just a metaphor of how I have sat with patients and Loved-ones during the time they were preparing to leave the living. This does not mean that you too must practice this model, I simply wrote of it to offer the concept only as a guide. Creativity is abundant in all of us, and uniquely we bring our own gifts to this process. Feel free to create your own sacred place of sharing life's ending with your Loved-one. Take time to create a sacred place in your mind's eye and try to practice the visual from time to time as you prepare to do this work. Only remember to remain true to your desire to bear witness to this person's ending and the beginning of understanding and acceptance.

Chapter 3

Receiving the News

I believe we would all agree that there are moments in our lives that seem to last for seconds, moments so brief ~ like catching the glimpse of a hummingbird in flight, that we wonder if they ever really happened at all. Then there are moments when time seems to stand still and we feel ourselves frozen, encased in a seamless cage of raging emotion unable to speak, to scream or to think. That gasping awareness that we have stopped breathing for that endless moment is our first coherent thought as we then begin to move further into the reality of what our senses begin telling us. It is a moment in time when the earth stopped moving. That moment is one encapsulated inside the pain of hearing devastating news.

Bad news, as they say, has a way of finding us. Whether it is a phone call in the middle of the night, a tear-soaked letter, or a conversation that begins with a troubled look, the result is a heartrending blow that begins an emotional chain reaction that begins to shift our reality and starts the process of permanent change in our lives. There is never any *right* moment to receive ill-fated news that a Loved-one has a terminal condition, yet it usually happens to all of us at one time or another in our lives. It is a moment in time that we would all rather do without.

Receiving the news that someone very special to you is going to die, is never easy. For many of us who receive the upsetting and unsettling news that a Loved-one's life is about to end, there is a physical and emotional sensation of numbness. The numbing sensation may be caused by the reality that you have finally heard the words you dreaded most. Or, it may be that you were just blind-sided and are incapable at that moment of wrapping your mind around this drastic news because you had no idea at all that this special person was ill. You might feel closed in, unable to think, to breathe, to speak or to move. Receiving this information may quiet you or ground you into an understanding of acceptance and peace. This difficult news might turn you away, cause you to shift focus and pretend it is not true, thus cloaking you in a state of denial, or it may launch you into orbit reeling in anguish and outrage. The possibilities of reaction are limitless.

There are no gracious moments during this time that may offer you much comfort or ease. It is a difficult time when a great deal is asked of you and it takes a greater amount of courage and discipline to be still, long enough to hear this type of news. It is an oxymoron in the works - your emotional being is fighting off the meaning of the words you are receiving, yet your mind and intellect want more and more information just so you can make sense of what you are hearing. As the difficult words enter your conscious mind, you may begin to notice that other parts of your body are not so willing to participate in this hearing. You may feel your knees get weak, or that your heart starts to beat fast and loud. You may begin to feel dizzy and light-headed if you are standing and find yourself moving towards a chair so that you may sit. All these physical symptoms are normal and directly related to the emotional shock that you are receiving. It is perfectly okay to be upset, confused, or even distracted in these moments following the news that someone you love and care about is moving towards death. The kindest thing for you to do in these moments is to care for yourself by not pushing yourself (which we all have a tendency to do) by trying to give more of yourself than possible at this particular time. It is a lot of hard work to absorb this kind of information and remain available to those you are sharing this moment with, or those who are requesting your attention else where.

Most often the initial reaction of receiving dreadful news that a Loved-one is terminal is either one of alarm, shock, despair and/or fear. In that moment you may balance precariously on the edge of your *own* cart-wheeling emotions (those of fear, dread and panic), *and* what you believe your Loved-one may be experiencing now that he or she is faced with an end-of-life prognosis. It is a frightening moment in time, and believe it or not, the fear, as real and harsh as it is, is perfectly normal.

Receiving the news that a Loved-one is about to leave this life as we understand it, a life that allows us the opportunity to participate in the sharing of worldly experience, communicating our feelings and emotions based on the exchange of thoughts, actions, and feelings, is now about to end creates an immediate reaction of fear. This *is*, however, a normal sensation that does *not* have to end in extreme heartache and unrest. Once you feel that you are aware of what you are facing – the imminent end of a life, it is okay to put a name to the emotions that come with that awareness. It may be Outrage or Terror. It may be Confusion or even Apathy. Whatever the name you give to your feelings, as long as you are being honest with yourself, there is no wrong emotion. If you find yourself in a quagmire of intense emotional unrest because you are realizing that you are going to be left alone without this Loved-one, you are perfectly within your rights to have those feelings too. Once again, by giving your feelings a name, you allow yourself a voice to share your feelings with those closest to you, and help define what you are experiencing. I will focus on this topic at length in chapter 5.

Receiving the news that a Loved-one is terminal is a moment in time when YOU are beginning your own battle through the fires of fear. This is an emotionally taxing moment in nearly everyone's life because so much is expected of you. There are so many words, feelings (both emotional and physical), questions and more questions at a time when very little is making sense. It is a time to practice listening and to trust that the passage of time will help you understand what it is that you must deal with.

Receiving the news that a Loved-one is dying is difficult, scary, heartbreaking and mind-bending. All these cascading emotions are okay, yet please just remember this.... Remember to breathe and to take enough time to be still so that you may honor your own thoughts and feelings by simply giving them names. If you chose, share your feelings with a trusted friend, and then take the time you need to move towards your Loved-one to begin the journey of Loving together.

Chapter 4

CHOICES

Whether you are prepared for the news or not, there comes a moment in time when you will need to make a decision regarding your own desire to participate in the support and caring of the individual who is dying. Yet hearing it, practicing the audio memory of that moment when you first heard the final prognosis over and over in your head, you may begin to get in touch with a deeper understanding that most always brings about intense emotion. This fearful reaction to the news, once spoken out loud, is a natural and honest one. Fear is second only to love, in that it has the ability to catapult any of us spinning out of control into a kaleidoscope of emotional turbulence within seconds. Once you enter the fear zone however, you lose control over the logical, sensible and practical responses you ordinarily rely on giving.

Throughout so many of life's experiences that offer us choices that we question, fear is the obstacle. Fear is the only barricade between your desire and wish to offer assistance in facing death together with your Loved-one. It is very important that you at least address this moment of choice with yourself before you go any further in building a bridge of support with this person who is dying. If you can honestly examine your motives and reasons for your choices regarding whether or not you may be of service to the physical and emotional needs of this person, you are surely being as truthful and honest as anyone could ever expect.

The choice you want to consider is, whether to be a consistent, on-going, physical presence of support through talking, holding, attending to physicals needs (like feeding or personal hygiene) or sharing quiet moments together with your Loved-one, or to be a behind-the-scenes support (which I will address later).

Supporting your Loved-one emotionally and physically in whatever way you feel most comfortable with simply by sharing time together is *not* about having an agenda and calling the shots as to what *you* need to talk about. It is not a time to discuss or address difficult topics that will ease *only your* mind during this time. Quite the contrary ~ it is about *being there* for this person to the full extent of meeting his or her needs at this time, and honoring the Loved-one's changing emotional, mental, spiritual and physical needs during this last phase of life. 'Being there' is simply being available to do what your Loved-one *needs*, through listening, caring, and sharing of your time, attention, energy and love. 'Being there' is unconditional support that is given from the heart, without expectation from the mind.

The choice to be present and available to the terminal individual, is by far, a great commitment, and is not for everyone. Remember, there are many other ways to offer loving support than to be physically and emotionally present to the dying. If you believe that your emotions will saturate your effectiveness by bringing sadness and heartache to this process because of your grief, then you may choose not to be an active participant, but more of a silent support through loving actions.

Being a behind-the-scenes support is also a very honorable choice for those who believe they are not emotionally prepared to deal head-on with the impending loss of a Loved-one. Choosing to be a silent support or a behind-the-scenes helper, is one who helps by aiding the Loved-one and family members with everyday household tasks. Choosing a role not to discuss the dying process is your right. Talking openly about death is not for everyone and that is very much okay. Please know this – we *all* offer gifts in any way we reach out to offer help through acts of kindness. Actions speak louder than words, and through your loving actions you may trust that you will make a great contribution during the last stage of your Loved-one's life. There are endless ways to help the dying and family members during this time such as organizing schedules and tasks, attending to home chores (grocery shopping, postal pick-ups, meal preparation, laundry, pet maintenance), making bill payments, appointments (medical, legal, auto), and yard and garden work. Loving someone to death does not mean that you must be physically present directly to the physical and emotional care of your Loved-one, but it does mean that you are supportive through kind and thoughtful actions that make life easier for your Loved-one and those involved with direct care service.

If it is your desire to be physically, mentally and emotionally present by choosing to support your Loved-one as he or she prepares to enter the final stages of living, you will need to prepare yourself for the cognitive, emotional and spiritual responsibility that will be expected of you. Begin by taking time away from the heartache you may be feeling at this moment. Try to clear your thoughts and calm your body, and sit still to reflect upon what it is you have always valued most about your relationship with your Loved-one. Although this time can be a sad time, try to think positively by focusing on the elements of the relationship you have shared together, and what you have always valued about it. Take your time to think it through. If it helps you to expand your thought process, share your reflections and memories with a close friend or family member so that you may get in touch with what it is that you have treasured and respected so much about this special person. Try to focus on what has been so important and memorable between the two of you. Reflect upon what has been *right* in your relationship, and practice reviewing those things that have brought meaning and joy to your life. What traits, experiences and memories do you value most about this person? Practicing positive memories you have about your Loved-one will be your greatest guide when trying to decide if you *will* choose to be mentally and emotionally present, and *how* you will support him or her through the dying process.

The choice, whether to be a front-line participant, or a behind-the-scenes contributor in the dying process, is completely up to you. Yes it is. Just remember, by taking time to think about what you can contribute positively to this special person, takes great time and attention to your own needs, versus the needs of the dying. In other words, this moment about *choice*, is all about you. Be patient with yourself, but above all, be honest and loving with yourself at this time. Do not dive in and trust that the answers will come as you stumble through this time with your Loved-one, yet consider that time is short, and that all you can truly give, is what you know to be true of your own ability to act during this most challenging time. Through the physical and emotional response of loving, caring and honest giving to the Loved-one, you will be able to receive comfort and understanding by accepting the fate of life's ultimate journey towards death, and to embrace it with dignity, faith and hope of continuing on without despair but instead, with gratitude and peace. Remember to trust in love. Loving yourself *first*, is the greatest gift of love that you offer to this process, and trusting in that will help you make the choice that will serve both you *and* your Loved-one at this time.

Chapter 5

Your Needs

When the time comes, and you decide to move onto the bridge and sit beside your Loved-one, you may begin to wonder what you can do for that person so that they may feel better. This is a very common thought, and a noble one. This is human nature at its best. Most of us, in one way or another, want to make things easier and be more helpful when trying to comfort another human being, and in the process, loose track of our own needs. We only see that person, and want to please and comfort him. This is a very natural and perfectly acceptable extension of our loving support when being present to one who is losing their time here with us. However, we must take care of ourselves too.

Addressing your own needs at this time is critically important for your own well-being. Taking care of *your* needs begins with the basics like eating properly, and getting enough rest. We all have so much more going on in our lives usually, that we tend to forget to nurture ourselves, especially through eating healthy and getting a good nights sleep. Scheduling your time is also another great matter to attend to as you prepare to spend some of your time with your Loved-one, meeting her needs. What you want to avoid is sheer physical, and mental and emotional exhaustion, in other words, stress. You body will readily tell you when it is feeling stressed through a variety of physical symptoms (headache, upset stomach, muscle tension or insomnia). Please pay attention to any signals and try to make positive changes that will allow you replenish your energy so that you can be and feel more productive.

When your thoughts and feelings begin to take hold of this new situation, you may begin to anguish over the thought that your Loved-one is going to die, and fearing what will happen to him and what he will go through. At this time you may not be thinking about what it is exactly that *you* are afraid of or struggling with. Fear has a way of creeping into *all* of our lives, day to day, or moment to moment. The fear we experience around loss, especially during a time when someone we love and care about is going to die, is a common state of being. It is purely a reaction, based on how we have come to understand what death means to us. Death means that you will forever be *without* this special and loved person. The reaction, therefore, is an honest one that is based on the fear of loss or abandonment of the person it is you love and care about. The questions begin to rise, "What can I do for him, now?" "Can I deal with this?" "What will I do without her?" "How will I go on?" "How will I survive alone?" So many questions and concerns begin to surface, and with them you will begin to expend a lot of restless or negative energy. The truth is, you may be concerned and fearful about your Loved-one's pain and dismal reality as she moves through this last phase of life, yet, it is *your* fear at this time that really needs to be addressed so that you are not creating more stress and strain in your life.

Taking time for yourself is essential to maintaining a healthy balance for your mind, body and spirit. This work, that of loving someone to death, is rarely done alone, and it helps to talk to a trusted friend or family member about what *you* are feeling. I cannot emphasis that "*you*" piece of this enough. How does one go about taking time for yourself? By going inward.

Taking care of your own needs is mainly about facing your own emotions, namely, your fears. What does it mean to go inward? It means simply to be honest with how you feel about what you are experiencing, and what you are afraid of. Do you feel anxious or worried about what more you can do? Do you feel uncertain as to your ability to help? Are you scared about being left alone? Are you worried about how others will be affected by this loss? Is this particular illness frightening to you? Are you fearful of how your life will change? Going inward begins with a choice to sit with these erupting fearful emotions and thoughts, and examine them. How? Quiet yourself, and allow your thoughts and emotions to surface so that you can put a name to what is going on inside of you. Journal your thoughts and write out your concerns, then approach them one by one. If you do this, and have written down your fears and concerns, and have named your emotions and worries, ask a trustworthy companion or family member to listen and support your insights, aloud. It is important to ask someone you trust that will impose no judgment on you as you reveal your inner most thoughts and feelings as they relate to this process. Having the freedom to share your thoughts and feelings, no matter what they are, will then begin to help you embrace and accept them one by one.

Sharing your grieving heart at a time like this is often a difficult task for most people, simply because it a very confusing time. At this time you are not only scared, hurt and angry knowing that you will be left alone without this special person, but also, you may be fearful of what your beloved must go through during this process. Remember, these are *your* thoughts and feelings, and you must be able to define them and *own* them. Often times what we feel emotionally, we tend to project onto others, meaning that we tend to think they too feel as we do. If you remain fearful and nervous, then those emotions will surely be reflected outward and onto your Loved-one. This fear-based energy will not only effect the Loved-one who is dying, but will also be set free on all others in your close circle of friends and family resulting in misguided intentions and misunderstandings. Sharing your fears can be difficult and at times a scary experience. What doesn't feel so simple, and in fact, what is difficult is the pain and anguish you will express as you become vulnerable allowing yourself to grieve openly and uncensored. It takes a lot of emotional energy to grieve, so take care of yourself by asking for support to share and express openly what is in your heart. For many of us, that is not an option as the consequences (embarrassment, shame, guilt) are much too threatening to face. You may fear that you may be judged, or that you will loose control, become enraged, panicked or depressed. But please remember, by giving a name to your fears, emotions, thoughts, judgments and feelings about what will happen to *you* when this Loved-one dies, you are able to self express and begin the process of freeing up your heart and mind in order to allow loving energy to help guide you through this process.

Ownership of feelings during a time like this is very important. Expression of these fears will allow you to become grounded in the understanding of what is real for you at this time, and what it is you resist and believe threatens your ability to be a loving, caring guide to your Loved-one. This is not intended to be a judgment [of yourself], just a window of opportunity to see yourself better and one that allows you to make a choice to express your fears about this experience so that you may begin to heal, thus promoting a pathway of positive expression and experience.

Another way of looking at this moment of reflection is that fears surrounding the impending death of a Loved-one are about loss and grief. Loss and grief are real and true emotions that are a natural part of this process. The fearful emotions that you may have worked so hard to push aside act as stonewalls in the pathway of giving and receiving in the experience with your Loved-one who is dying, and serve only to create more stress and strain to you both physically and emotionally. Asking for and using the support of family, friends or clergy is a main ingredient in managing your needs at this time. Self-love is granted when you chose to sit and examine what is going on *inside* yourself. Taking care of your own emotional needs at this time, is about respecting *your own* process of giving your time and attention to another who is about to die. Taking care of your needs by seeking support at a time like this, is absolutely necessary.

Loving someone to death begins with self-love, that of understanding one's own truth, by pushing through the fear, to serve and honor the process of death with this person who is about to leave this world. The emotional experience of pre-grief is a complex maze of body and mind sensations that are preparing you to get ready to exchange real time with a Loved-one, for memories that you once shared with a Loved-one. Grief too, is a process, yet it often creeps in silently and roots itself firmly in our souls. Taking time to listen to the inner voice of unrest within you, will allow you to get in touch with what you are feeling.

While being present to and for the dying, it is so very important to take time to listen to what is going on inside of your own heart and acknowledge any physical changes. There may be days when you feel tired and distracted, quiet and calm, or rattled and nervous. There may be days when the tears arrive and seemingly do not end, or the sensation is numbness. There may be days when depression is there, waiting by the bedside pushing you back, robbing you of your power and effectiveness. These sensations are real, honest and all a part of this process. When you begin loving someone through their process of dying, you will be experiencing many emotions, and many of them may feel very heavy and dark. It takes a lot of personal strength and energy to give your positive attention to your Loved-one, not to mention the other people in your life. During this time you must remember that you are not a wind-up toy wearing a perm-a-press smile and reciting non-stop niceties while you bestow your good nature without end. Oh no! You are a *real* person who has a great deal of real life experiences to deal with day to day in addition to facing your impending loss. Yet while all of this is going on, you are also experiencing a sense of grief. So often, most of your time and attention with your Loved-one will be focused on her needs and your grief will be silent. In fact, you may never even be aware that the anguish and sadness that you are experiencing is grief, until you begin to share it with a trusted confidant, and examine the way it affects you. It is *your* process, and *you* are entitled to the full range of emotional experience. I only ask that you take care of your emotional self periodically by finding healthy and safe avenues to express whatever you need to, in order to free yourself from the negative weight of what you may experience. Again, this is not to say that everyone who is reading this will feel negative emotions throughout this experience, this is only to offer guidance of how to let go of those thoughts and feelings that bind the spirit.

Loving someone to death is a selfless act that will challenge the best of us to examine our own personal issues around death and dying. It is often a time when you will be greeted with the desire to "make your peace" and at times, wish to reveal the hurt in your heart to your Loved-one regarding your past relationship. As a caregiver to many individuals I have loved through this process including family, friends and patients, I ask gently that if you *do* decide to resurrect past histories of heartache and sorrow, be well advised to honor the choice your Loved-one makes regarding *his* choice *not* to engage in the sharing of this topic of conversation. This is the right of the dying. I would also request that you not take this time to reveal grueling expressions of personal conflict that you may feel a need to release and to ask the advice of your Loved-one to help you resolve. Relationship issues are common, and you may be triggered into seeking counsel from your Loved-one regarding a personal issue you may have had with your Loved-one, or concerning other relationships that you have been struggling with or are in conflict with, but please keep in mind that is what your support network is there for. However, if you do go ahead and ask advice regarding old wounds, and are rejected by your Loved-one because her choice is *not* to discuss the matter, I ask you to be patient and loving, of yourself and your Loved-one, and to do your best to let go of this inner conflict while in the company of your beloved. Practicing loving regarding and patience will serve to allow you to trust that this is now a turning point to offer unconditional love as an opportunity to grow stronger and wiser in the process of accepting death. While it is true, that sharing feelings is a powerful way for people to grow closer, love and heal, it is also true that at this time the focus of *all* subject matter of discussion, is very important. If you do have the need to express personal expressions of conflict, it will serve you greater to discuss these issues with friends, clergy or family members that will help guide you to resolutions that will help you quell any desperate desire to expel them to the Loved-one who is beginning to face his or her own personal challenges of dying.

Death is now inevitable, and your choice is to either

act through a loving caring heart that opens all doors to understanding, forgiveness and truth, as opposed to expressing personal heartache of past events. By trusting this process, choosing love, you will be very surprised at how quickly your personal baggage regarding past experience will be gently lifted away, and in its place will be a new offering of understanding and resolution that will bring you and your Loved-one the connection that your heart desires most.

Once again, it is so very important that while you are loving this special person to their death, that you continuously remember to sort out your own feelings, identify them, and talk about them with a trusted friend or family member. Remember, this piece is about *you*, recognizing and addressing what *you need* is the first step to being an effective caregiver to your Loved-one. Untangling your physical and emotional knots, from time to time will assuredly help you focus and practice your loving attention as you sit together upon the bridge while offering comfort and calm to your Loved-one during the difficult process of dying.

CHAPTER 6

THE NEEDS OF THE DYING

The first question on everyone's mind is, "What do I *do* for my Loved-one when we are face to face, and alone?" This is the most honest response you can possibly have at a time like this. This is also a time when your own fears around the issue of death and dying have their greatest tendency to be projected outward leaving you scared and clumsy when trying to start the conversation about meeting his or her needs at this time. Being out on the bridge, feeling nervous and afraid to talk about what is happening with a Loved-one who is slipping away from life, is a natural and normal response from a new caregiver. Having addressed your own personal concerns about what has been churning inside of you, you are now ready to face the next task, that of addressing the needs of your Loved-one.

When it comes to those Loved-ones who are consciously aware and have lived with the knowledge that death is inevitable, there is an understanding of why you both are here. In the case that it is a child, or a Loved-one who does not seem to grasp an awareness or understanding that death is coming, the conversation regarding what is needed must be gentle, thoughtful and focused on the immediate moment. I would like to offer my own personal insight here and share that it has been my experience and is my belief, that young or old, any individual who is facing inevitable death, *does* have a sense of this experience on some level, whether it is outwardly acknowledged, or not. Even though death is the issue, it need not be the focus. The expectation does not have to be on death, but instead, must be on living. Simply because your Loved-one *is* among the living, just as you are, and must be treasured and honored in that place until death arrives.

The needs of the dying are the first priority. If you are willing, try and learn all that you can about the illness that your Loved-one suffers from. This information will serve you well and will help guide you in the direction of caring for him or her, especially if you choose to help with meal and/or personal hygiene needs. Having a clear understanding of your Loved-one's condition, can also help you adjust your schedule around periods of rest and have a better understanding of behavioral changes due to any effects of the medication he or she may be on.

The need of the dying may also be emotional, spiritual, or mental. As you know, and will bare witness to from time to time, these needs will be met by different people, at different times. You must never feel that it is *your* sole responsibly to meet every single need in every single moment for your Loved-one, as that is not possible or even practical.

For the person who is facing death, visits from family and friends are so very important. Often times the visit is the highlight of their day. Every one of us brings different gifts at different times to the Loved-one who is dying. Trusting in our own unique ability to make a positive difference, rather than try to accomplish tasks and actions that we have little expertise in, allows us to offer a moment of love, kindness and joy. Stick with what you know. If you have the ability to offer a relaxing visit, perhaps a back-rub or foot message ~ that gift will always be greeted and accepted with sincere gratitude. Touch is a basic human need that all too often gets overlooked. Touching is a wonderful expression of love and care and can certainly help soothe weary bones, achy muscles and tired feet. Please remember to ask your Loved-one if it is okay with him or her to touch them if you want to give a gentle massage, because sometimes there is pain associated with the pressure of touch depending on the physical condition of your beloved. If you offer the gift of laughter, that too will surely be appreciated for all its weigh in distraction from the difficult nature of this process. Visits of all types lend time to disconnect from the serious nature of dying. Visits are as different as those individuals who take the time and energy to sit with a Loved-one who is terminally ill. From story telling to board games, reading to card playing or letter-writing, to errand hopping or cooking and cleaning, the gift is the spirit of *being there* for this person in need.

When considering a visit, it is best to make arrangements through either the Loved-one or any other person or family members that may be overseeing the daily needs of the individual. It is a big help to have your name placed on the calendar for a specific day and time as your Loved-one and other family members and friends also require times for visits.

Physical needs of the Loved-one take special priority as they are meant to ensure comfort and secure dignity to the failing health of the individual during this time. Again, attending to physical needs is not for everyone. Healthcare practitioners and/or a chosen few family members and friends that are safe, caring and loving step in at a moments notice to assist the physical needs of the dying. Physical needs can and often do change dramatically over time when illness is progressive; therefore it is always good to have a skilled individual in attendance. If it is your desire to assist in the personal hygienic care, or even offering assistance in feeding, it is important to ask questions and watch carefully for any signs of distress or discomfort of your Loved-one. If you are unsure about something, just ask. Remember that those individuals facing death may feel very passionate about maintaining control over their life, after all it is still theirs to control. By asking questions, this simply act of kindness, allows your Loved-one full control to offer *you* assistance through providing informative information, and therefore usually results in a feeling of actively participating in life. This can be a very good experience for both of you as it deepens the level of trust, communication and understanding between you.

Emotional, spiritual and mental/intellectual needs of the Loved-one are also very important and should be continuously monitored to ensure that they are met. There are a variety of ways in which these needs can be met, yet the starting point begins with awareness. Many individuals who are facing death still chose to live their lives and are capable (to some degree) to participate in daily living experiences and wish to converse with the world around them. Some individuals may enjoy catching up on the current events of friends or news events from around the world through newspapers, phone calls, letter writing or dictation. Your Loved-one may want to listen as you read to him, challenge you to a game of chess, or watch a favorite program together with you. Perhaps your Loved-one will express a desire to continue to follow a current passion, such as needle-point, painting, playing an instrument or listening to music. All these needs are important as they are mentally and emotionally stimulating, and deserve the caregivers loving attention to each request, and above all, to their safety.

The needs of the dying come in as many different shapes and forms as there are different types of people. For some, being held and wanting to be lovingly touched may be a craving that not only works to soothe their aching muscles, but also helps them feel closer to the caregiver. Some individuals who are nearing death never want to be touched, and that should simply be respected too. Always remember, when in doubt, ask.

Each person based on their life experience has different needs. Your personal connection to the Loved-one also comes with specific conditions surrounding how needs be met. This is a matter of dignity and comfort, as there are levels of trust and safety within each relationship. Learning as much as you can about the illness helps you to determine your level of interaction when addressing physical and (sometimes) emotional needs. Remain open and loving, ask questions to others who also offer assistance in areas of care-giving that you are unsure about and love, respect and patience will be your guide to how you will meet the needs of your Loved-one.

CHAPTER 7

STARTING THE DIALOGUE

One of the obvious concerns of sitting with a Loved-one who is dying, is, "What am I going to say?" This is a very normal concern. Very few of us are schooled in this course of talking about what is going on, as we contemplate having a conversation with a Loved-one that we just discovered is dying. Well, you need not worry, because talking *about* what is going on, (death) is not necessary to starting the conversation.

When death is the issue, we crumble. Many of us are not taught how to be *okay* with the subject of death, or dying. In fact, we are taught, mostly, that dying due to an aggressive illness or a brief yet life-threatening illness or a serious accident, is to be feared and resisted. This is exactly where those fears will defeat you when you step onto the bridge and wish to begin a conversation, even with your very best intentions. The topic of conversation does *not* have to be death. Why? Because the person that you are loving is not dead, *and* because this person may *not wish* to discuss this subject at this time, or ever. Although this may seem strange and awkward to read....remember, dying at this time is not *your* process, and just because you are now there, ready to be of service in emotional support of your Loved-one during this difficult time, it is the life of this individual that is being honored and respected. Attitude, approach and understanding, *is* everything.

Starting the conversation with a Loved-one while you are together on the bridge does not have to be difficult. Start from where you are. Chances are good to excellent that if you are reading this book it is because you want to be present and available to love someone that is special to you while they are facing death. If this person is someone who is special, it stands to reason that you have a relationship with this person. Based on that, you have a starting point.

Starting where you are means, talk about what you feel most comfortable with. Choose topics that are familiar to both of you, those that were always a part of your relationship. Many, many times, the conversation begins with simple easy expressions of everyday events, and certainly those things that you can do for your Loved-one. It is truly okay to talk about the weather too, even though you might think that this is not the time to talk about something so trivial. It's perfectly okay, as it is very familiar, and just a way to start talking. Relax ~ having very casual conversations at first, is a wonderful way to build trust and safety.

Even though you may have a long-term relationship with one who has recently been diagnosed with a terminal condition, it is reasonable to except that things can change when news of a terminal condition is received. We all have our own way of hearing and filtering the news that life is ending, and because of this, it is also reasonable to expect that the person who is now facing their own mortality may have his or her own way of understanding, accepting and self-expressing their feelings on this subject. Be prepared for changes. This is so very important to internalize and accept because the simple truth is, receiving ill-fated news has a way of creating change in people.

At times this type of news is weighted in on-going, conflicting emotions for many people, which must be respected no matter who the individual is because he or she may choose not to open up to a conversation regarding their demise, ever. It may that your Loved-one will not only refuse to address the subject, but continue on as if nothing at all has changed. This is perfectly okay, and simply must be honored. Or perhaps your Loved-one may wish to talk about his or her impending death every time you visit, or with (in some cases) *anyone* who will sit and talk about this experience. Speaking about this issue depends on many factors, such as physical well-being ~ whether they are tired, feeling ill, or emotionally drained or upset. The choice of whom they speak to about their process, and when, is strictly up to them, and should be honored.

There are several ways that the conversation can develop when you are sitting with and beginning a dialogue with a terminally ill person. And there is really no way to predict which direction the conversation with your Loved-one will go, as this process is so deeply personal for everyone. There are many factors that affect this personal choice, and I simply ask that you respect whatever choice they make, as well as the physical condition they are in. I would like to outline a few perspectives regarding end-of-life conversations, and offer some guidance as to how to maneuver through them.

To begin with, people are characteristically positive or negative in nature and their approach to life usually reflects that. This is the old, "the glass is half empty" or, "the glass is half full" perspective. For those individuals who see the glass as half *full*, there are a couple of scenarios in which the conversation might take place.

For some Loved-ones, the conversation will remain about living. There are many easy-going gentle souls who also have a glass-is-half-full appreciation for life which may reflected in either a great zest for life, or a quiet appreciation for living. They will remain focused on things they know, have enjoyed experiencing and will take comfort in knowing that *your* presence will offer them solace in the on-going events of your life, and theirs. These individuals are those who choose to focus all of their energy on living, and never, *ever* discuss death or dying with anyone. Not only will they not discuss it, they may even appear to you that they are unaware of their prognosis as they remain calm and relaxed and happy. The truth is, is that this is an amazing event and opportunity to simply listen and ask thoughtful questions regarding your Loved-one's beliefs and wishes during this last phase of life. Remember, the focus of questions does not have to be on death, but on *life*, and keeping in mind that this journey is not yours, and that it is not for you to control the direction of the discussion. At times like these it is so very important to practice respect in honoring the needs of the dying by remaining supportive and attentive to witnessing any and all choices, especially those the Loved-one wishes to express.

Do not let the choice of your Loved-one to discuss anything but death discourage you. If their choice is to keep the conversation light and away from the tragedy of dying, embrace that, and allow the conversation to remain just where they feel most comfortable. This choice, remember, is not about you, but about them. Often times individuals who do not talk about the inevitable do so because they are not ready or willing to self-express about this topic. That is perfectly okay, and should be well respected. Just being there upon the bridge, sharing time and space and attention is just exactly what they want at this time. Remember that most often the dying do not often choose to speak about this process with everyone who walks through his or her door for a visit.

Another way in which the conversation might flow is that which fully and openly involves death and dying, the whole experience. Some Loved-ones who are open-mined and embracing of life may also be embracing of death, and feel very free and easy to discuss the topic of their impending death with you, or anyone for that matter. These individuals may speak about death with an ease and openness that often times helps those surrounding them feel lighter and more grounded in this experience. Loved-ones may share fears, wishes, opinions, concerns and desires all related to the dying experience. At times the pathway of conversation may take you into uncharted lands where you may begin to feel energized and open to the discussion and you may both feel a freedom and ease of discussing any and every possibility of what is to happen as death approaches and arrives. Your Loved-one may begin asking questions and seeking answers of what is to happen next (after death). He may ask for your own personal insights and beliefs regarding life after death and may feel a need to discuss his own thoughts and ideas as well. This is perfectly okay. However, remember to give these questions careful consideration of your time and attention. Just allowing an open space for your Loved-one to speak openly about whatever they need to express is a true and wondrous gift of love that you grant while remaining present and attentive. Or, you may find yourself beginning to feel fearful and unsure as to how to respond to this dialogue. If you discover that your are feeling nervous and confused as to how to share in the conversation regarding their impending death and find yourself withdrawing either silently or by shifting the focus of the conversation back to a more comfortable (for you) subject, its okay, this too is normal....just try to relax. However, if you are truly feeling ill at ease, be gently honest about your feelings. It would be kinder to disengage from the conversation with integrity and honestly, than to allow yourself to sit in discomfort creating a negative energy that may result in misguided intentions and discomfort for the both of you.

For those Loved-ones who see the glass as half *empty*, there are also a number of ways they may approach the subject of their dying process. Sometimes a terminally ill individual who often appears closed off, anxious and fearful may be very eager to discuss everything they are experiencing while they are so ill. This person may wish to discuss all aspects of their impending death because they are so afraid, worried and scared about what is happening to them, and what will happen to them as time passes. They could become very needy and dependent on a care-giver who they converse with on this subject and their focus on dying could easily become emotionally draining to you or other care-givers. Your Loved-one might become distracted, concerned or fearful. These behavioral characteristics are also normal and appropriate considering what they are facing. Their concern may be for family members, children perhaps, or they may be wondering what will happen to them day-by-day or week-to-week. They could be afraid of the unknown and wondering what happens *after* death, or be concerned that there is something they may need to do before the end.

Unfinished business is a very important factor in the dying process, and can be a very important topic to discuss with your Loved-one. Whether your Loved-one is accepting of death, or resisting, if you are simply aware of and recognize conversation patterns that relate to this topic, it could shed a great deal of light in a very dark corner. It is okay to ask a Loved-one, in a gentle and caring way, what they believe and feel they would like to do, or finish (if anything) before they become too ill to do it. It could be something simple like reviewing photo albums, re-reading old letters, or writing letters, making phone calls or with assistance take a drive to the beach, watch a favorite movie or have their favorite food from their favorite restaurant. Offering your assistance to help your Loved-one realize a goal she had is a marvelous opportunity for both of you at this time, as it strengthens the bond of trust and support.

An angry, mad and otherwise negative tempered individual may have a very clear understanding of his or her prognosis, but never once admit or acknowledge that they are dying, and grumble on as always. This person may appear to be in disagreement with the medical prognosis, or in denial of what is actually happening to him. This Loved-one may simply choose to continue to keep to his own way of doing things, and his own beliefs without asking or wanting any discussion to the contrary. You may feel conversationally cast away from any discussion regarding his condition, but please remember, it is *his* process and he gets to lead when it comes to discussing his condition, namely, the topic of death.

Some individuals, who are of a pessimistic mind-set, may not change in their approach to life at all by remaining gloomy and cynical, yet they may decide that they *want* to die, and chant their desire to die to you, or others who may sit beside them. This can be quite distressful, and at times frightening, especially if your Loved-one becomes fixated with dying. Sometimes, people who are faced with their own mortality become very hostile and guarded. Their anger is rooted in fear, yet they express it in so many difficult ways, sometimes by verbally asking to die. They may lash out by yelling or crying, or even pleading for death. Or, they may become defensive regarding their state of health and refuse any attention from those individuals who only seek to love, comfort and care for them. Again, this can be a part of the dying process as it is a very personal journey and one that must also be respected. If you share your time listening without judgment, and practice loving kindness in allowing your Loved-one to lead the discussion, no more can be asked of you.

Please remember, your Loved-one is moving through his or her own process, and must always be treated with respect and loving regard. What they are seeking most is comfort and safety from those care-givers that they share they fears and concerns with. Just by listening and gently reflecting back their concerns will give them the support that they are looking for by being witnessed and listened to, knowing they are heard through sharing what they are thinking and feeling at this time. If at any time you become disconnected emotionally by feeling uncomfortable, please ask for help and guidance from another close friend or family member of your Loved-one, so that your Loved-one is consistently upheld with tender care and loving regard no matter what state of mind he is in.

Throughout the course of conversing, sometimes the level of conversation may be light and carefree, and at other times it may be sad and melancholy. I believe that whatever the emotional level of the conversation and topic, there is always a story unfolding. Remember, that the most consistent gift, no matter what the topic, is to be the most attentive and interested audience ever! Always ask simple and appropriate questions, and only offer your own reflections when it is appropriate or specifically asked. This is not to say that you must always keep the conversation rolling exclusively about them, because keep in mind, this is not a confessional. All I am suggesting is that this is a time when many words will be spoken on many levels, and it should be at the direction, pace and design of the individual who is crossing that bridge from life to death.

During this time, physical changes will be taking place and with those physical changes, often time emotional and cognitive changes take place as well. Personality changes in our Loved-ones may be extreme, predictable, reasonable, or there may be no changes at all. It is worth mentioning here that it is entirely possible to experience changes in attitudes, disposition and a Loved-one's nature at this time. The following is a list of possible changes you may encounter.

Your Loved-one may become quiet and reserved. You may notice that after experiencing an ease of conversation regarding his condition, he suddenly may not want to discuss what is going on with his illness or discuss anything that has to do with his physical condition at all. Again, this is his right, and he is the only one who can make the decision regarding whether or not he wants to talk about it. Instead, your Loved-one may wish to discuss everything that represents normalcy, people, places and events that he has always felt connected too, before the terminal prognosis.

After having experienced a "no discussion" policy, your Loved-one may suddenly become very open and expressive about the process of dying. She may want to talk about what it means to be dying, all the time. For some care-givers this news might be a big surprise, but again, it is *her* process, *her* journey, and only *she* gets to make the choice regarding how much she wants to open it up for discussion. And, she may have a lot of questions, fears, hopes or requests. She may even seem overwhelmed with the prognosis she was given and the only way to work through it is to talk about it.

Some individuals change their personalities in midstream by becoming gentle and embracing, when before the prognosis they were not quite so open. They may be peaceful, positive, joyful, willing to explore the newness and what comes next. In fact, they may even be enthusiastic about this journey. Remember, whatever the personal approach by the Loved-one, it is *their* call, and no matter what, it should be respected and honored, and never challenged.

When death is pending, it is possible that an individual who was once always outgoing, casual and open in their conversation, may suddenly appear shut-down, closed off or non-responsive, or even angry and rude. Sometimes this is due to the nature, course and the severity of the illness as well as the medication they are taking. Their unresponsiveness may also be due to depression, a characteristic that is also not uncommon at a time like this. Whatever the behavior, whether it has changed drastically or is shifting ever so slightly, it is so very important that you honor the process as dying is a very personal experience. Some wish to share it, others do not. Some wish to grow and evolve to a higher level of consciousness, while others may just stay steady-on-course to their accustomed way of thinking, feeling and acting and disclosing. Some may even choose to move headlong into the conversation about death so fast, that it creates a disturbance among all those committed to caring and loving the person, causing alarm and distress with cascading emotions that may leave you nervous and fearful. Please remember, that this time is never easy and is a complicated journey for all.

There may be a time during a conversation when your Loved-one may say something very dark and upsetting for you to hear, regarding his or her process of dying. Many times people who are aware that death is emanate, and who are struggling with health issues, may grow weary of spirit, as well as body, and tell you that they want it all to be over with, meaning, they want to die. They may be very persistent and certain as the weight of the illness becomes insufferable. The most normal impulse when this happens is to say something like, "Oh, please, you don't mean that!" Please, *please* try to refrain from saying such things as it removes the individual from a place of truth and expression. By listening and staying there to love and support your Loved-one, even with talk of wanting to die, you are honoring their right to their feelings and beliefs. You don't have to agree, you simply need to honor their right to express their own personal truth. This is a powerful testimony to the reason you are there ~ to love! Rather than try to redirect their talk of wanting to die or ending their life, try simple reflections, something like, "You sound very certain about what you want," or "It must be very difficult to deal with this illness." As you show interest in what your Loved-one believes, thinks and is feeling, you are sharing very intimate moments of truth and understanding. It really is okay to ask questions about their feelings, or process, when they self express their desire to die. When you are at this level of communicating, take it slow, and let your Loved-one lead you. Many people are very grateful to answer your questions inquiring about their personal thoughts, beliefs and feelings at a time like this. Asking questions, gently, is a very loving gesture, and yet it requires only compassion and the willingness to listen. There may be a moment also when your Loved-one asks *you* about your own thoughts, feelings and beliefs on death and dying, or what will come after. Sharing your beliefs will allow the bond to deepen, but be prepared to give the conversation back to your Loved-one, and continue to open your heart and mind to what you are hearing and learning....as there is much to learn.

One of the danger zones while listening to your Loved-one speak about his or her process is to say, "I know how you feel." This is more of a habit, and certainly can never be the truth..... because you are *not* this person, and you *cannot* experience this transition from life to death from the place where you are sitting at this time. Unless you have ever experienced the process of dying, it is best to try to refrain from using phases that make it sound like you share an experience like this one. Just because you *understand* the feelings your Loved-one is describing, *doesn't mean* you are *sharing* the feelings.

There may be many times when your Loved-one is not able to talk, or just does not wish to carry on a conversation. Let him or her know that it is perfectly okay with you, and remember that silence is also a wonderful opportunity to show your love and support. You can watch television together, read, look at photos or pray together. Just simply sitting by the bedside of your Loved-one while sleeping, will offer you an abundance of gratitude as your awareness of this person's experience deepens during your time together.

Lastly, know when it is time to leave during each visit. This will challenge you in many ways with fearful thoughts of wondering if you will have more time together. This is also a very normal thought process. That is why, while you are together, you must *make every minute count* by loving and caring for this very special person. By being aware of your time together and making each moment count, you are working through your own process of what is yet to come. As I have stated, and will state again, this experience, although extremely difficult and sad at times, *will* change into something else. This experience will change your life as you reflect on the sincere and loving contribution you gave to this person's life.

Chapter 8

The Final Chapter

The final chapter of life is what at I have been writing about, what you have been asking questions about, thinking about, and even participating in ~ loving someone to death. Death is the final bow. It is what is expected and feared…all at once.

When death is approaching, there are many changes that begin to take shape right in front of you. I will briefly mention the physical changes, and those that take place on the emotional-mental-spiritual level. Yet please keep in mind, the focus must always remain on the dignity and integrity of the person who is dying, no matter what physical, mental, emotional or spiritual changes occur.

During the final hours, there are physical indications that death is near. Since the body begins a natural process of shutting down, the body will begin to cool, and there will be a change in the breathing pattern, even congestion may occur when breathing becomes labored. The individual may begin to refuse food or water, and if you insist they should take even small amounts of water, your Loved-one may become further agitated and uncomfortable. The Loved-one may become restless, irritated, lose consciousness or drift in and out of sleep. As the body begins to relax, bodily fluids may be expelled without awareness from the individual, a normal process that must be met with respect and compassion with the focus on preserving the dignity of the Loved-one.

During this final phase, you may begin to experience your Loved-one detaching from you or becoming unresponsive and withdrawn. This can be a difficult event for most people who are supporting and loving a person who is dying, yet this is a necessary part of letting go for the Loved-one. Please keep in mind that during this time the Loved-one can still hear you and many sounds in the room. It is a great act of love and comfort to speak softly and lovingly, tenderly touching your Loved-one, and saying whatever you can to help them let go.

Your Loved-one may also exhibit behaviors related to emotional, spiritual and mental experiences. Your Loved-one may appear to speak with, or to look to someone they believe they are seeing in the room who is not there. This is a normal part of the transition, and even though you are not sharing this experience, it does not mean that it is not a very real experience for your Loved-one. The dying see many things, and openly communicate with persons they believe and sense are with them at this time. This is perfectly natural, and should simply be respected as part of this process. Continue to comfort and speak to your beloved with loving attention to honor this process, so that your Loved-one will not become afraid.

During this time when life begins to ebb away, a Loved-one may slip in and out of a conscious state. Often times a Loved-one will move through the entire process of dying without ever regaining consciousness. For some caretakers this is a most distressing experience, while for others, they consider it a quiet blessing. Even in this sleep-like state, sounds can still be heard. Speaking softly, gently stroking the hand or face is a tender act of love that has been proven to reach inside even the most unresponsive patient. The ability to give freely of your heart and mind to the needs of your Loved-one as they move towards the end of life is the foundation of unconditional love.

Death does not always come peacefully, yet there are kind and loving gestures we can do to help our Loved-ones during this time. Often times a Loved-one will be very near death, but also very restless and seemingly searching. It can be a time of high anxiety for those of us who are there watching, waiting and willing to do something, anything.....but often times we just don't know what that is. This is the part where we, the ones who have cried and ached at the witnessing of life ending, now give permission to our Loved-one to let go. Often times a Loved-one will try to hold on for a number of reasons, but typically this requires so much energy that the Loved-one becomes increasingly uncomfortable. Giving your Loved-one permission to let go, is one of the most deeply, loving acts of kindness and respect imaginable. Most often the Loved-one will hear this message and begin to relax and move closer into death.

This is also the time to say your good-byes in the way that is most like you. It is perfectly okay to cry, or tenderly hold your beloved, kiss them or even thank them. There is no template of what you are expected to do, just do what is right for you, right from the heart.

As the Loved-one leaves the place of the living and has passed, there are still levels of awareness for this person, and it is perfectly okay to continue speaking softly, gently hold or continue rubbing his or her skin. Taking time to be there, present and attentive, especially at the every end is such a great testimony to the life of the departed. Almost every hospital or nursing care facility will honor and respect the gathering of family members and dear friends that have remained with the departed Loved-one by granting a quite space and time for crying, hugging, saying last goodbyes, and experiencing the silent avalanche of new grief.

This experience ~ that of feeling new waves of heartache as well as relief, will then begin a new process for you to step through. That step being, to gather yourself to express your final good-byes and then to leave. This step is one of the hardest of all, and only needs to be met with patience and self love, as there is once again, no template of how this is done. As I said previously, remember to breathe, and to trust in what you know, and what you love. You are now leaving the bridge, and your Loved-one has also left, both of you in opposite directions, and for you, life *will* go on.

CHAPTER 9
LIFE GOES ON

After the passing of a Loved-one, the world seems to change instantly for most of us. When the news is sudden and unexpected, our emotional sensations imprison us in countless ways – denial, anger, shock....the range of feelings are beyond measure. For those of us who had the opportunity, and it *was* an opportunity, to participate in the ending of life by being there for a Loved-one, that time too is riddled with its own rip-tides of emotion. The moment of walking away from your departed Loved-one after he or she has died, is an emotional event most people do not take time to talk about, let alone even think about. From that instant of lifting your body to leave the departed and walk towards your own life, you will notice that life is now different, once again. Be very gentle with yourself at this crossing, as a lot of emotions may surface and leave you feeling depleted and frozen inside the experience you are now leaving behind. This is perfectly okay, just take your time and honor your own process.

Grief is a human condition that is normal and natural. Grief comes to us *because* we have loved. There will be times in every life where the grief we feel after a loss will just consume us, but please, let the passage through grief lead you ever so slowly to a healing and realization of what life is meant to be ~ appreciated and lived to the fullest. Be patient and loving with your grieving heart, and take moments to reflect upon your experience with your Loved-one, with someone who will listen to all your words. This too is a time of honor and respect as grieving the loss of someone can be a very difficult and seemingly never-ending journey. Remember to trust in what you know and what you believe in as you move through this rights-of-passage to the next launching of what life has in store for you.

Moving forward is what life is meant to be, and we can do this without dishonoring the special person we loved to death. This is a time to sift through your thoughts and emotions of what this past experience has meant to you and taught you about your own life. Your life does go on, and one of the greatest gifts you are about to embrace and set free all at once, is that of what your Loved-one gifted you with while you two were together during this last phase of life.

From this time onward, you will reflect and review so much of what transpired between you and your Loved-one, words or no words, the experience over time will reveal its meaningful content and will allow you to internalize it so that you may share your insights and discoveries with those you choose will gain from your experience. Please don't underestimate this event in your life, what you just gave of yourself was a tremendous gift to humanity and will continue to open new pathways of discovery to you, and others, simply because you experienced it. Not everyone has this opportunity, or chooses to take the opportunity to be there for someone who is dying. The gifts you have received are in your knowing that you made a careful consideration to be there and participate in the ending-of-life for someone you loved. Praise yourself and offer your gratitude to your departed Loved-one for all that you have experienced. This is indeed, a most noble and humbling experience for any one of us to encounter. Remember, a life is not ended if the memory of that life is kept alive through our commitment and sincere desire to recount the special moments we shared with our Loved-one.

THE AUTHOR

Lou Bacon began working as a direct-service volunteer for a Hospice organization in southern New Hampshire in 1994. She has consistently greeted each individual that she was asked to support through their dying experience, with a gracious spirit and positive warmth that has allowed each patient to take full control of their dying process. Lou has kept her focus on the needs of the individual, her own needs to promote positive care-giving, and has faithfully practiced the skills she has learned that would bring hope, love, respect and honor to the process of dying.

Lou teaches at the college level, practiced as a mental-health therapist, runs bereavement support-groups, personal empowerment workshops and is highly accomplished in the art of presenting soft-skills instruction.

Lou welcomes your insights into this process of caring for and loving people into their deaths, and can be reached at LJBacon@gmail.com.